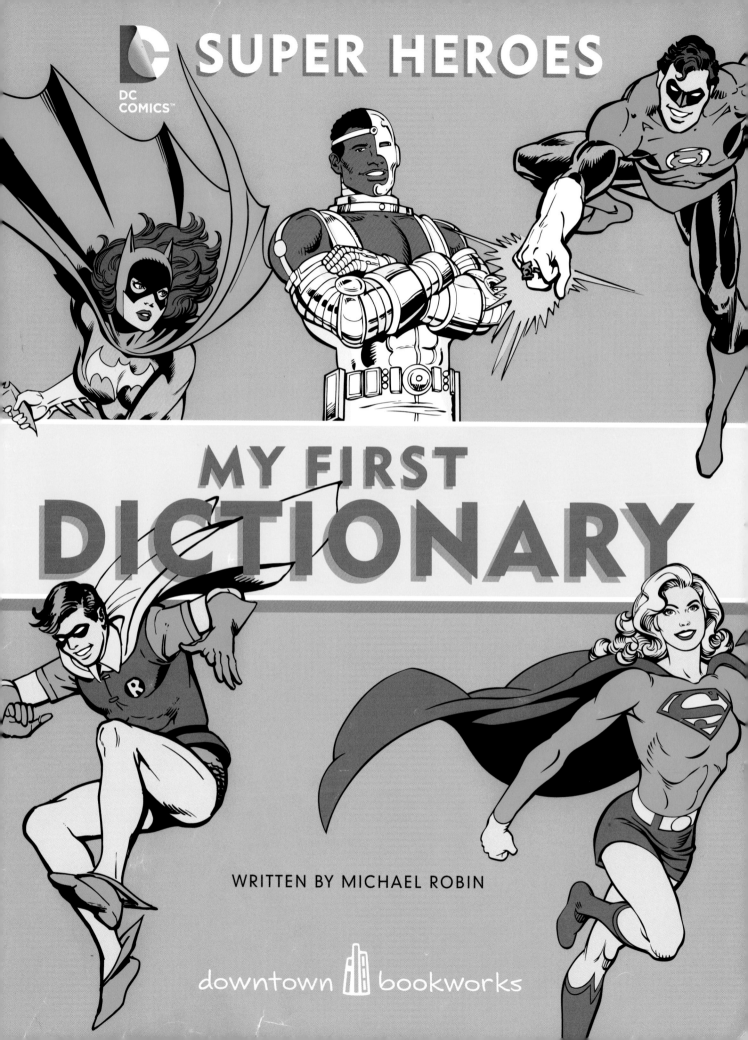

Designed by Georgia Rucker Design
Typeset in Geometric

We would like to thank the following illustrators whose artwork appears throughout the book:

Jack Abel
Murphy Anderson
Ross Andru
Dick Ayers
John Beatty
Tex Blaisdell
Wayne Boring
Rich Buckler
John Byrne
John Calnan
Ernie Chan
Vince Colletta

Dick Dillin
Terry Dodson
Kieron Dwyer
Mike Esposito
Duncan Fegredo
Ramona Fradon
Joe Giella
Dick Giordano
Sid Greene
Mike Grell
Don Heck
Carmine Infantino

Gil Kane
Stan Kaye
Karl Kesel
George Klein
Joe Kubert
Bob Layton
Pablo Marcos
Jose F. Marzan
Sheldon Moldoff
Irv Novick
Kevin Nowlan
Jerry Ordway

Charles Paris
Al Plastino
George Roussos
P. Craig Russell
Bernard Sachs
Mike Sekowsky
Bob Smith
Dick Sprang
Curt Swan
Anthony Tollin
Keith Williams
Tom Ziuko

Printed in the United States of America
July 2014
ISBN 978-1-935703-86-0
10 9 8 7 6 5 4 3 2 1

Published by Downtown Bookworks Inc.
285 West Broadway | New York, NY 10013 | www.dtbwpub.com

TABLE OF CONTENTS

HOW TO USE THIS BOOK

A dictionary tells you what different words mean and how they are spelled. This dictionary uses pictures to show you the meaning of words. Some of the words are common things that you see and say every day. You will also learn about many of the DC super heroes, their friends, and even some super-villains.

The words are organized by letter. A is the first letter of the alphabet, so A words go first, then B words, and so on.
You will see a big letter at the beginning of a new letter section. The letter for that section also appears on the side of the page.

cage
This tiger is in a **cage**.

cake
Superman arrives at the party with the world's biggest **cake**.

calendar
A **calendar** is good for keeping track of important dates, like birthdays, holidays, and more!

camera
Lois Lane takes pictures with her **camera**.

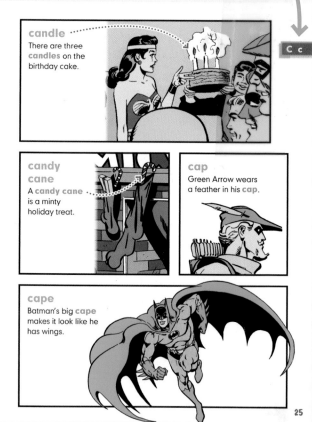

candle
There are three **candles** on the birthday cake.

C c

candy cane
A **candy cane** is a minty holiday treat.

cap
Green Arrow wears a feather in his **cap**.

cape
Batman's big **cape** makes it look like he has wings.

Each word appears in **blue**, and then it's described in a sentence where the word appears again, in **green**.

Teen Titans
The **Teen Titans** are just as strong and brave as the grown-up heroes.

teeth
Aquaman's smile is bright because he never forgets to brush his **teeth**.

television
Bruce Wayne and Dick Grayson watch a news report on **television**.

te nis
...e Flash is ...st enough ...o play **tennis** against himself!

tent
Superman flies high above a circus **tent**.

through
The Flash has the power to pass right **through** solid walls!

tiara
Wonder Woman wears a golden **tiara** on her head.

throw
The Flash can **throw** a baseball at super-speed.

tiger
Animal Man dances with a wild **tiger**.

tilt
Batgirl's motorcycle **tilts** to one side.

T t

105

Sometimes you will see an arrow pointing to the item in a picture.

You can read this book from beginning to end. Or you can look up a specific word or DC character. To find a word or character, you'll need to know its first letter. Then turn to the beginning of that letter section. You can see where each letter section starts in the Table of Contents on page 3.

Happy reading!

THE ALPHABET

A B C D E
F G H I J K
L M N O P
Q R S T U
V W X Y Z

above

Superman holds the car **above** his head.

adopt

Jonathan and Martha Kent **adopt** baby Superman and love him as their own son.

afraid

Billy Batson is **afraid** Black Adam will catch him.

YIKES!

after

Shazam! flies **after** Black Adam.

ahead

The red car is **ahead** of the green car.

airplane

Regular people have to fly in an **airplane**.

alien

Martian Manhunter was born on another planet. He is an **alien**.

almost

The Joker **almost** squirted Batman with his trick flower!

always

Superman will **always** catch Lois Lane.

THANKS, *SUPERMAN!* I ALWAYS KNOW I CAN COUNT ON YOU!

anchor

An **anchor** is dropped from a ship to the ocean floor to hold the ship in place. This anchor was dropped on the ship's deck.

animal

Beast Boy can turn into any **animal** he can think of.

Aquaman

Aquaman can talk to sea creatures...and swim like one too!

archer

An **archer** knows how to use a bow and arrow.

argue

Supergirl and Zatanna **argue** over a Yeti. Even friends disagree sometimes!

HE'S MINE!

NOT ON YOUR LIFE!

armor

Batman notices something strange about a suit of **armor**.

around

Elongated Man stretches his arms all the way **around** three green creatures and The Flash.

artist

Superboy drew a picture of himself. He is a good **artist**.

Atom

The **Atom** is the world's smallest super hero.

away

Superman throws two rocks **away** from Earth and toward the stars.

B

baby
When Superman was a **baby**, he came to Earth in a rocket.

THUD!

back
Batman's **back** has lots of muscles.

backpack
You can carry lots of useful things such as books or snacks in a **backpack**.

backward
Superman will catch this man before he falls over **backward**.

bad

The Joker, Sinestro, Bizarro, and the other super-villains are **bad** guys.

balance

Aquaman **balances** on the backs of two dolphins.

bald

There is no hair on Lex Luthor's head. He is **bald**.

ball

The baby picks up a desk so he can get his favorite **ball**.

> ME LIFT DESK AND GET RUBBER BALL UNDERNEATH!

balloon

This lucky girl has three super hero **balloons**.

barbecue

A **barbecue** is an outdoor grill for cooking things like hamburgers and hot dogs.

barrel

Green Lantern uses his power ring to lift four **barrels**.

baseball

The Flash holds a **baseball**.

baseball bat

A baseball player swings his **baseball bat**. Crack! Home run!

CRACK!

bat

Bats love to fly at night.

Bat-Signal

When people need Batman's help, they shine the **Bat-Signal** in the sky.

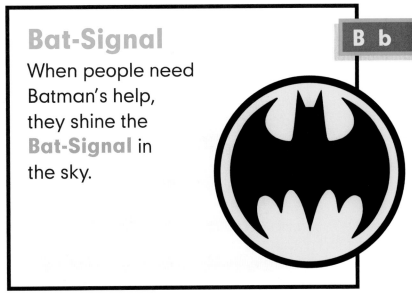

Batcave

The **Batcave** is Batman's secret hideout underneath his house.

Batgirl

Before she was **Batgirl**, Barbara Gordon was a librarian!

Batman

Batman is sometimes called the Dark Knight.

Batmobile

Batman built the **Batmobile** to be the fastest car on the road.

beach

Wonder Woman's home, Paradise Island, has many sandy **beaches**.

bear

Look out for that angry **bear**, Kid Flash!

RRRR

before

Robin climbs down **before** Batgirl.

beg

A little dog sits up to **beg** for treats.

behind

What's that noise? Green Lantern turns his head to look **behind** him.

below

Gotham City's buildings and bridges are **below** Batman.

between

Aquaman is **between** Wonder Woman and The Flash.

bicycle

A boy rides away on his **bicycle**.

Billy Batson

Billy Batson is the young man who can turn into the mighty Shazam!

bird

A **bird** sings in a cage.

birdcage

The best place for the Penguin is a **birdcage**!

bite

No crocodile is quick enough to **bite** Wonder Woman.

Bizarro

Bizarro always does the opposite of what Superman would do.

Black Canary

Black Canary is an expert martial artist and motorcycle rider.

block

With a superpowered push, Superman knocks over a line of **blocks**.

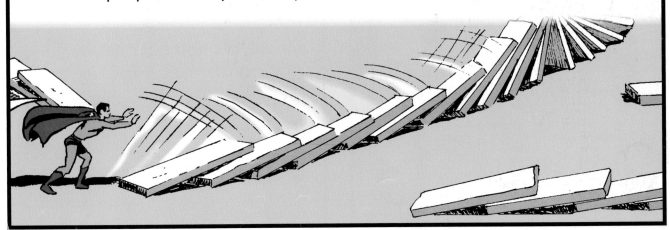

blow

Ma and Pa Kent watch their adopted son, Clark, **blow** out a fire with one blast of breath.

book

The library is a great place to find a **book**.

bone

Superman forgot to turn off his X-ray vision. He can see his friends' **bones**!

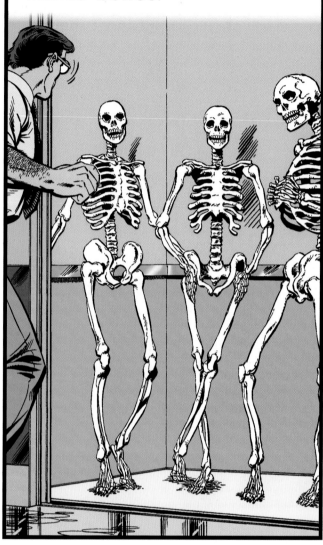

boot

This is Poison Ivy's **boot**.

bored

There's nothing to do on Mr. Mind's home planet, so he feels **bored**.

BOR-ING!

bottom

Can you see the **bottom** of Batman's boot?

bounce

Batman's Batarang **bounces** off the Penguin's umbrella.

bowl

The Flash eats soup from a **bowl**.

box

The Joker thinks it's funny to pop out of a **box**.

boy

Aqualad is a **boy**.

bracelet

Wonder Woman's magic **bracelets** protect her.

break

Superman can **break** even the strongest chain.

bridge

Captain Cold and Mirror Master run across a **bridge** made of ice.

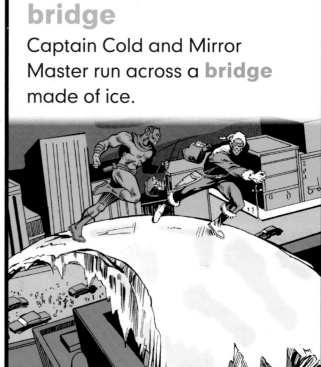

broom

Lois Lane flies through the air on a magic **broom**.

Bruce Wayne

Don't let anyone know that **Bruce Wayne** is secretly Batman!

bubble

Aquaman leaves a trail of **bubbles** in the water.

building

Superman flies past the tall **buildings** of Metropolis.

bull

Wonder Woman rides a **bull**.

buried

Superman smiles even when he's half-**buried** in snow.

bus

Thanks to a lift from Superman, this **bus** won't be late.

C

cage
This tiger is in a **cage**.

cake
Superman arrives at the party with the world's biggest **cake**.

calendar
A **calendar** is good for keeping track of important dates, like birthdays, holidays, and more!

camera
Lois Lane takes pictures with her **camera**.

candle

There are three **candles** on the birthday cake.

candy cane

A **candy cane** is a minty holiday treat.

cap

Green Arrow wears a feather in his **cap**.

cape

Batman's big **cape** makes it look like he has wings.

car

Superman lifts a **car**.

card

The Joker likes to leave playing **cards** at the scene of the crime.

carry

A giant monster **carries** The Flash in his hand.

carousel

This **carousel** doesn't just spin around. Thanks to Superman, it also goes up!

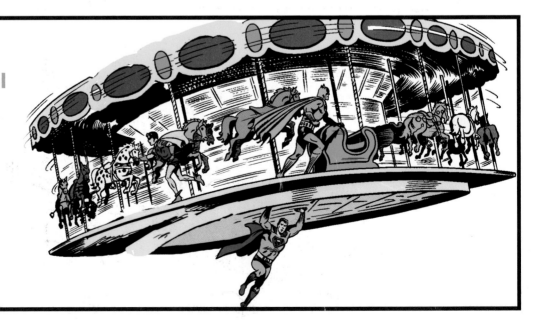

castle

This orange **castle** makes a safe headquarters.

cat

Streaky is a super-**cat**.

Catwoman

Sometimes **Catwoman** is nice and other times she is not so nice.

chair

Lex Luthor sits in a **chair**.

change

Bruce Wayne **changes** out of his regular clothes and into his Batman costume.

charge

Green Lantern has to **charge** his ring, or it runs out of power.

cheer

The Amazons **cheer** for Wonder Woman. She's saved the day again!

chess

The Flash and Despero play **chess** with super hero–shaped pieces.

chin

Darkseid touches his **chin** with his hand.

city

In a **city**, people live and work close together in tall buildings.

Clark Kent

No one guesses that mild-mannered reporter **Clark Kent** is really Superman.

claw

Look at this Parademon's sharp **claws**.

climb

Robin can **climb** this steep wall.

close

Batman's face is very **close** to the Joker's.

clock

Robin flips past a giant **clock**.

THAT CORNERED CROOK PUSHED *ROBIN* OFF THE TOWER-TOP...

CATCH, ROBIN!

GOT YOU!

cloud

Supergirl flies high among the **clouds**.

club

A **club** is a group of people who all like the same thing. The boys in this club all like Superman.

coin

Two-Face flips a **coin**: if it's heads, he acts naughty, and if it's tails, he acts nice.

cold

Wonder Woman feels **cold** in the snow.

color

There are costumes in many **colors** in Batman's closet.

comic book

Comic books tell stories about super heroes through pictures.

Commissioner Gordon

Commissioner Gordon is a brave lawman who helps Batman.

cook

Uncle Dudley **cooks** eggs for Billy Batson.

I LIKE 'EM *SCRAMBLED,* UNCLE DUDLEY.

SCRAMBLED... HARUMPH! OF *COURSE,* DEAR BOY.

cover

Doctor Fate's helmet **covers** his whole face.

cozy

The baby looks **cozy** wrapped in her orange blanket.

crawl

Superman digs a tunnel for his friends to **crawl** through.

crib

A **crib** is where young children (and sometimes super heroes) sleep.

crocodile

A **crocodile** is a big reptile with sharp teeth.

crooked

Metamorpho has turned himself into a **crooked** slide for this woman to ride.

cross

Wonder Woman **crosses** her arms in front of her chest.

C c

crowd

A **crowd** of people cheers for The Flash.

HERE COMES THE FLASH! HOORAY!

crush

Superman's hands **crush** a stone into sand.

KRUNNNCH

cry

Babies **cry** when they're hungry or tired.

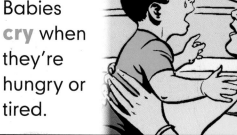

curl
Plastic Man **curls** around a lamppost.

Cyborg
Cyborg is part man and part machine.

D

dance

The Fiddler's magic music makes two super heroes **dance** like puppets!

decorate

This van is **decorated** with purple flowers.

desert

There's no water to be found anywhere in this hot, sandy **desert**.

desk

Commissioner Gordon works late at his **desk.**

Diana Prince

Look closely at **Diana Prince**. Can you tell she is Wonder Woman in disguise?

different

These two pictures of Batman are not the same. They are **different**. Can you see how?

dinosaur

Wonder Woman holds on tight. She's caught a very large **dinosaur**!

dive

Aquaman **dives** into the sea.

dizzy

Don't spin too fast or too long or you'll feel **dizzy**!

dock

The Flash runs along a **dock** where boats come to shore.

Doctor Fate

Doctor Fate has magic powers.

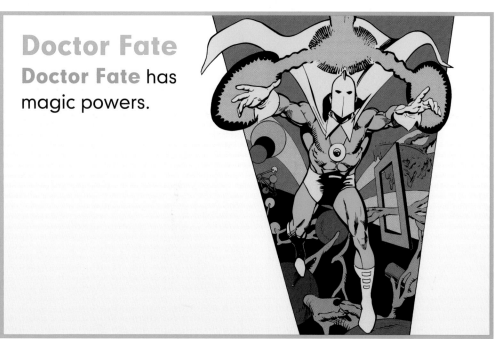

dog

This **dog** watches The Flash and Kid Flash run by.

down

Clark Kent walks **down** the stairs.

dress

This big kid knows how to **dress** himself.

drive

Sometimes Batman lets Robin **drive** his car.

drop

Oops—that woman **dropped** a dish!

E

each

A man holds something in **each** of his two hands.

eagle

An **eagle** perches on Wonder Woman's wrist.

Earth

Superman flies around and around our planet, **Earth.**

eat

Clark Kent is so full from his meal that he doesn't want to **eat** any more pie.

egg

In the henhouse, Ma Kent watches her son collect **eggs** at super-speed.

elephant

This charging **elephant** is surprised to bump into Animal Man.

elevator

Superman doesn't always leap to the tops of tall buildings. Sometimes he takes an **elevator**!

Elongated Man

Elongated Man is one of two stretchy super heroes in this book. Can you find the other?

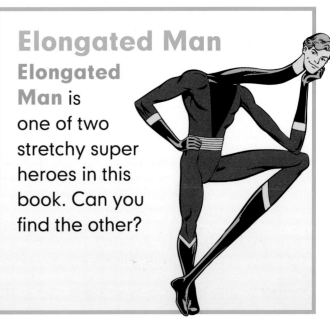

enjoy

Wally West **enjoys** meeting his favorite super hero, The Flash.

every

Batman has captured **every** one of these villains.

excited

People feel **excited** when they see a super hero fly by.

eyeglasses

Superman wears **eyeglasses** to trick everybody into thinking he's Clark Kent. Can you tell this is the same person?

F

fast

The Flash is so **fast** that he can finish any job in no time!

feather

Hawkgirl's wings are covered with **feathers**.

fence

Outside the farmhouse is a bright, white **fence**.

ferry

This old-fashioned **ferry** is a boat that carries people and cars across the water.

firefighter

Firefighters are heroes too!

fire hydrant

Firefighters connect their hoses to **fire hydrants**.

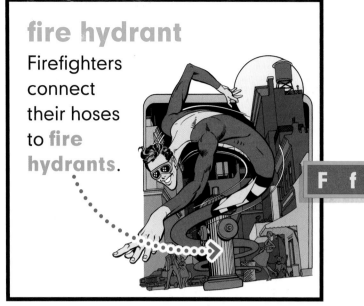

F f

fire truck

A **fire truck** takes firefighters wherever they are needed.

Firestorm

Firestorm is sometimes called the Nuclear Man.

first

Batman jumps out of the car **first**.

fish

These **fish** live in the ocean. They might be Aquaman's neighbors!

fishing rod

You're supposed to use a **fishing rod** to catch fish, not people!

fix

When the Batmobile is broken, Batman and Robin **fix** it.

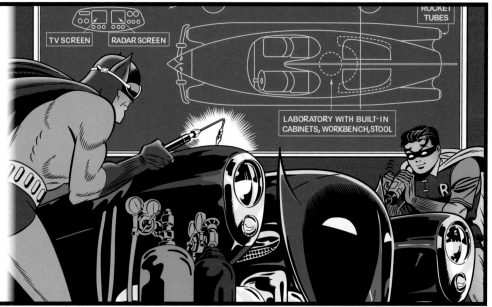

flag

Superman holds the **flag** of the United States.

flashlight

Robin uses a **flashlight** to find his way in the dark.

The Flash

The Flash is sometimes called the Fastest Man Alive.

flippers

Mera wears **flippers** on her feet so she can swim even faster.

F f

float

Crates **float** in the water behind a soggy Clark Kent.

fly

Lots of super heroes can **fly**.

follow

Creeper **follows** Star Sapphire out into the night sky. He is behind her.

food

The Flash catches the **food** before it lands on the floor.

footprint

The Flash and Kid Flash wonder who could have made such a big **footprint**.

force field

Green Latern makes a **force field** with his power ring. The force field is a wall of energy that protects him.

Fortress of Solitude

The **Fortress of Solitude** is Superman's secret hideout near the North Pole.

forward

Doctor Fate reaches his arms **forward**.

frightened

Some people look **frightened** when they see a super-villain.

funny

Batgirl and Robin make **funny** faces.

friend

Batman and Superman like doing things together. They are **friends**.

F f

fruit

Figs are a sweet kind of **fruit**. Apples and bananas are other kinds of fruit.

fur

Gorilla Grodd is covered in **fur**...but don't try to pet him.

G

game
Two men play a **game** of cards.

ghost
Is that a **ghost**? No, it's a bad guy under a sheet!

gift
Wonder Woman gets a very special **gift** from her mother.

girl
Batgirl and Supergirl are **girls**.

give

Lois Lane **gives** a package to Clark Kent.

glow

The magic in Wonder Woman's lasso makes it **glow** with golden light.

good

Superman, Batman, and their friends in the Justice League are **good** guys.

good-bye

Shazam! and Superman wave **good-bye** to each other.

49

gorilla

He may look like a regular **gorilla**, but Grodd is actually a super-smart super-villain.

Gotham City

Batman keeps watch over his hometown, **Gotham City**.

grass

The green **grass** is up to Animal Man's knees.

Green Arrow

Green Arrow has a trick arrow for every occasion.

Green Lantern

Green Lantern is a peacekeeper who patrols the stars.

G g

grow

Plastic Man can make one leg **grow** longer than the other leg.

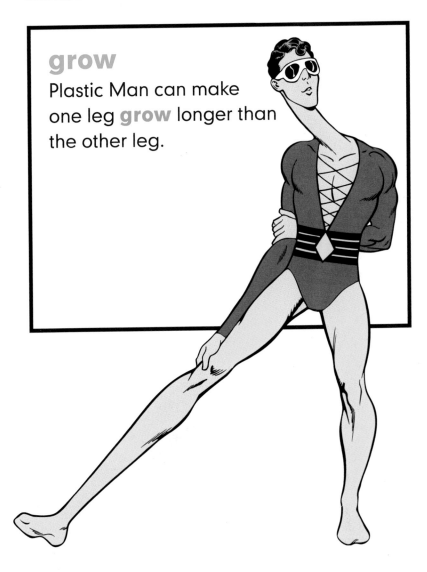

grumpy

Robin feels **grumpy**. Even super heroes have bad moods sometimes.

H

hair

Hawkgirl and Mera both have orange **hair**.

haircut

It's hard to give Superman a **haircut** without breaking the scissors.

half

Half of Wonder Woman has been turned into wood, but the other half is ready for action!

hamburger

Captain Boomerang has a **hamburger** for lunch.

hang

The Dynamic Duo **hangs** from a helicopter.

hat

Harley Quinn wears a silly **hat** on her head.

heat vision

Superman uses his **heat vision** to melt things with his eyes.

Hawkgirl and Hawkman

Hawkgirl and **Hawkman** come from the planet Thanagar.

helicopter

Batman's **helicopter** is called the Batcopter.

helmet

Black Manta can breathe underwater because of his special **helmet**.

help

Green Lantern **helps** Superman catch Brainiac.

hero

A **hero** is a brave person who helps others.

hide

The Joker and the Penguin **hide** when they don't want anybody to know where they are.

high

Green Lantern flies **high** above Coast City's buildings.

hill

The Flash runs up and down the **hills**.

hold

Two super hero babies **hold** hands.

hole

Superman punched a **hole** through the wall.

hood

Raven's **hood** covers part of her face.

hop

A bunny **hops** to safety.

55

house

Supergirl flies away from her **house**.

hose

A masked man sprays water from a **hose**.

hot

Watch out! Fire is **hot**!

hot dog

Superman walks by the **hot dog** cart.

hungry

Hungry birds want to fill their tummies.

I

I i

Ice

Batman and Robin try to stay warm inside these blocks of **ice**.

ice cream

Children cheer when Wonder Woman brings **ice cream**.

inside

Robin sits **inside** the cockpit of Batman's plane.

57

instrument

The Fiddler's violin is an **instrument** that is used to play beautiful music.

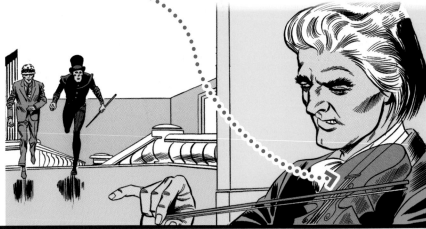

into

Batman jumps **into** the Batmobile.

invisible

People can't see Wonder Woman's jet. It's **invisible**.

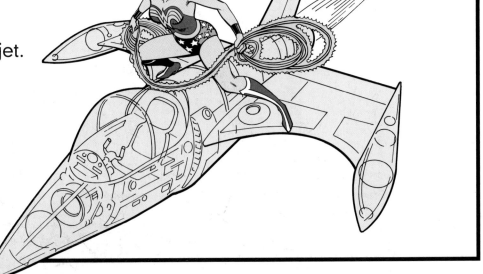

J

jaguar

A **jaguar** is a big jungle cat that is covered with spots.

jewelry

Super-villains are always trying to run off with **jewelry** that doesn't belong to them.

Jimmy Olsen

Jimmy Olsen doesn't know that his friend Clark Kent is really Superman.

joke

A good **joke** makes everybody laugh.

HA! HA! HAR! HA! HO!

Joker

The **Joker** is sometimes called the Clown Prince of Crime.

judge

After a super-villain is captured, a **judge** decides his punishment.

jump

Wonder Woman can **jump** very high.

Justice League

When these super heroes team up, they call themselves the **Justice League**.

K

kangaroo

Wonder Woman bounces into action on a **kangaroo**.

key

A **key** is used to open a lock.

kick

Robin and Batgirl **kick** their powerful legs.

kid

The mighty Shazam! is secretly a **kid** named Billy Batson.

Kid Flash

Kid Flash is a speedster like his friend and teacher, The Flash.

kiss

Robin gives Batgirl a friendly **kiss** on the cheek.

kitten

A **kitten** licks Supergirl's hand.

kneel

Robin and Batgirl **kneel** on the ground.

knot

There is a **knot** in Wonder Woman's lasso.

Krypto

Superman's superpowered dog is named **Krypto**.

Krypton

Superman was born on **Krypton**, a planet that had a red sun.

K k

Kryptonite

Kryptonite is a glowing green rock that makes Superman feel sick.

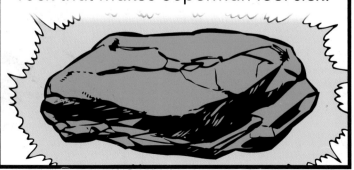

L

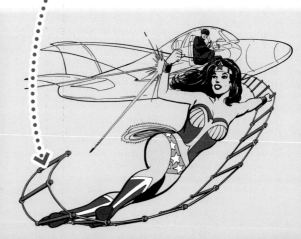

ladder

Wonder Woman climbs a rope **ladder** to her Invisible Jet.

lake

Elongated Man rests next to a blue **lake**.

lasso

Wonder Woman has thrown a **lasso** around Cheetah.

last

Green Arrow is behind the other super heroes. He is **last**.

laugh

The Joker loves to **laugh** at his own jokes.

leaf

Poison Ivy cares about every **leaf** in the forest.

lean

Catwoman **leans** to one side.

Lex Luthor

Lex Luthor uses his incredible brain power to battle Superman.

lift

Green Lantern is powerful enough to **lift** a mountain.

light

Light shines from the windows of these buildings at night.

lion

Superman tames a **lion**.

listen

Children **listen** while Wonder Woman reads them a story.

little

The Atom is a very **little** super hero.

Lois Lane

Lois Lane is a fearless news reporter—and Superman's number one fan!

L l

loud

Cover your ears when a noise gets too **loud**.

long

Elongated Man has a very **long** neck.

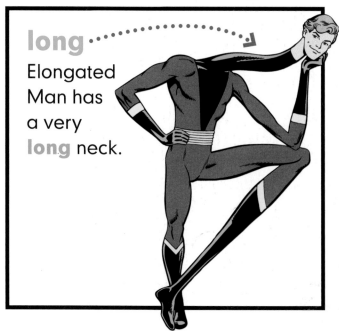

M

mail

Barbara Gordon reads a letter that arrived in the **mail**.

mailbox

To send a letter, put a stamp on it and drop it in a **mailbox**.

many

There are **many** Green Lanterns.

Martian Manhunter

Don't be fooled by **Martian Manhunter's** fierce face. He has a kind heart.

Mary

Mary is a member of the Shazam! family. Just like her brother, Mary gets her powers by saying the magic word, "Shazam!"

match

The Penguin and the Joker both wear striped purple pants. They **match**!

melt

When Superman forgets to turn off his heat vision, his glasses get too hot and **melt**.

mess

Catching super-villains often means making a **mess**.

Metropolis

Superman lives in a big city called **Metropolis**.

middle

Wonder Woman is in the **middle**. Batgirl is on the left, and Supergirl is on the right.

mirror

Lex Luthor likes to look at himself in the **mirror**.

money

Oops! Someone dropped a bag of **money**.

moon

A bright full **moon** glows in the sky behind Batman.

motorcycle

Robin's **motorcycle** is called the Redbird.

move

The Flash makes a car **move** by waving his arm super-fast.

muscle

Aquaman has big **muscles**.

N

N n

nest

A **nest** is a bird's home.

net

The Riddler is trying to catch someone in a **net**.

never

No matter how fast they run, these villains will **never** get away from Green Lantern.

newspaper

Superman knows what's going on in the world because he reads the **newspaper**.

next

Batgirl has just landed on the street. Robin will land **next**.

nice

You can tell from his friendly smile that Shazam! is very **nice**.

N n

Nightwing

When Dick Grayson grows up, he stops being Robin and becomes **Nightwing**.

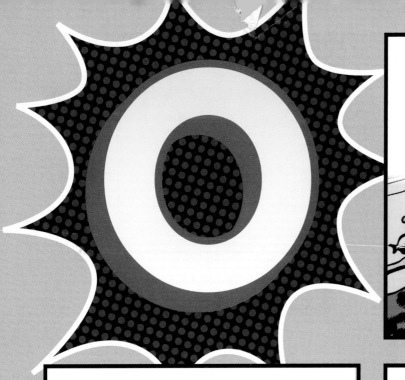

oar

An **oar** is used to make a boat move.

ocean

Most of our world is covered by **ocean**.

octopus

An **octopus** is a sea creature that has eight arms.

on

Wild animals stand **on** Green Lantern's big green square. Next stop: the zoo!

oops

Oops! Oh well, everyone makes mistakes!

open

The Joker's mouth is usually wide **open**.

or

Should Robin run through the "Out" door **or** the "In" door?

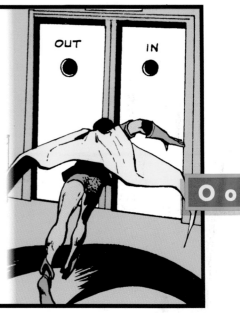

ostrich

An **ostrich** is the biggest bird.

ouch

Ouch—that hurt!

KA-RAAASH

out

Mirror Master throws his loot **out** the window.

outer space

Green Lantern can fly among the stars in **outer space**.

outside

Robin, Superman, and Elongated Man are **outside** the buildings.

O o

P

paint
Paint comes in many different colors.

pajamas
This super hero sleeps in polka-dot **pajamas**.

paintbrush
You can make a work of art with a **paintbrush**.

paper
A pencil and **paper** are all you need to draw a picture.

Paradise Island
Wonder Woman grew up on **Paradise Island**.

P p

party

A **party** is a fun celebration.

pass

Super heroes **pass** pieces of cake to one another. Everyone remembers to say "thank you!"

peek

A villain **peeks** through a window at Commissioner Gordon.

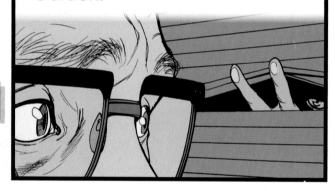

pencil

Clark Kent keeps a cup of **pencils** on his desk.

pet

Krypto is Superman's superpowered **pet**.

picture

Five villains pose for a **picture**. Everybody say "cheat!"

piece

One punch from Superman breaks a big stone into little **pieces**.

pigeon

Superman and Lois surprise the **pigeons**.

piggyback

Elongated Man gets the world's fastest **piggyback** ride!

P p

plant

Poison Ivy sits on a very big **plant**.

Plastic Man

Plastic Man is one of two stretchy super heroes in this book. Can you find the other?

play

A group of boys **plays** football.

playful

Krypto is in a **playful** mood.

point

Robin **points** to show Batman where to go.

police car

Lex Luthor is being put into a **police car**!

police officer

A **police officer** tells Superman where to find the bad guys.

polka-dot

A girl wears **polka-dot** pajamas.

pool

It's fun to cool off in a swimming **pool**.

porch

Animal Man and his wife sit on the front **porch** of their house.

power ring

Green Lantern imagines things, and his **power ring** makes them appear!

proud

Barbara Gordon feels **proud** when she wins an award.

P p

pull

Workers cheer as Superman **pulls** their vehicle out of the mud.

push

Superman **pushes** the train back, so it doesn't go off the tracks.

Q

question mark

The Riddler's costume is covered with **question marks**.

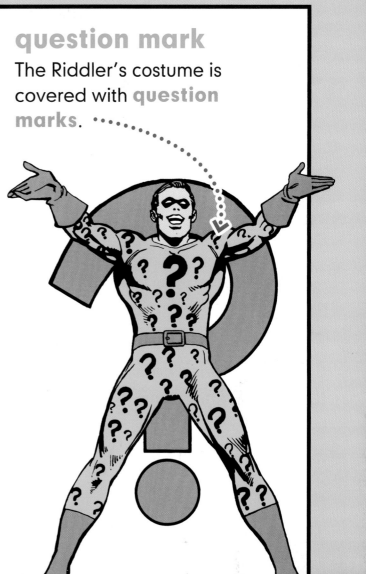

Q q

quick

The Flash is so **quick** that he passes a speeding taxi as though it's standing still.

quiet

The library is a **quiet** place where we use indoor voices.

R

rabbit
Superman can't believe his eyes—he's on a world full of talking **rabbits**!

race
Superboy is winning this **race** with a train.

racecar
A **racecar** is made to go very fast.

rain
The **rain** gets everybody and everything wet.

rainbow
Hawkman flies through the **rainbow**.

R r

ray

A strong energy **ray** blasts out of Firestorm's hand.

reach

With his body stretched out long, Elongated Man can **reach** high into the sky.

GOT IT!

read

Superman **reads** a note.

ready

Batgirl is **ready** for another lesson from Batman. He teaches her self-defense moves.

R r

Red Tornado

Red Tornado can turn his body into a whirlwind!

relax

Even super-villains need to **relax** sometimes… and a big comfy chair is just the place to do it!

85

reporter

A **reporter** tells the world about important news.

restaurant

Friends eat together at a **restaurant**.

riddle

A **riddle** is a tricky question that is hard to answer.

ride

Robin **rides** a motorcycle.

rip

There are many **rips** in Batman's costume.

Robin

Robin, the Boy Wonder, is Batman's partner in fighting crime.

R r

robot

Brainiac is a **robot**, a machine that looks and moves like a person.

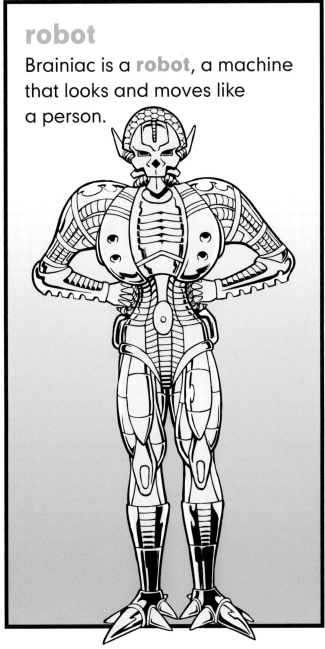

rock

When Aquaman wants to stay dry, he stands on a big **rock**.

roll

Plastic Man turns into a wheel and **rolls** into action.

rocket

Baby Kal-El rides a **rocket** to Earth.

R r

87

roof

The Flash runs right over a building's **roof**.

rope

Batman holds onto a **rope**.

R r

round

A full moon is perfectly **round**.

run

The Flash can **run** faster than anyone.

S

sand

In the desert, The Flash makes a whirlwind of **sand**.

scissors

Robin knows to be careful when using **scissors** for cutting.

scold

Mary **scolds** her brother for making a mistake.

scream

Black Canary has a powerful voice called a sonic **scream**.

S s

seahorse

Aquaman rides a giant **seahorse**.

sea star

Superman is careful not to step on this **sea star**.

secret identity

Many super heroes disguise themselves as regular people. That is their **secret identity**.

see

Wonder Woman smiles when she **sees** Paradise Island.

serious

Batman rarely laughs or smiles. He is a very **serious** super hero.

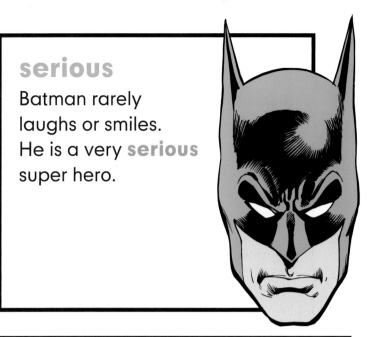

shadow

Do you see Batman's **shadow** on the wall behind him?

shark

Sharks circle around Batman and two other men.

Shazam!

Shazam! is sometimes called the World's Mightiest Mortal.

S s

shelf
A scientist puts a bottle on a **shelf**.

shine
Green light **shines** on Hal Jordan's face as a power ring chooses him to be its new

shirt
Superman takes off his white **shirt**.

master.

ship
A **ship** is a large boat.

shoe
Commissioner Gordon's **shoe** is brown.

shop
Pa Kent sells things in his **shop**.

shovel

A big green **shovel** is just what Green Lantern needs to clean up Gorilla Grodd's mess.

shrink

The Atom can **shrink** so small that you can't even see him.

side

The Flash runs down the **side** of the building.

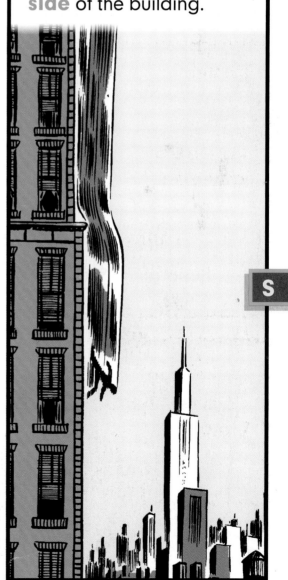

sidekick

A **sidekick** is a super hero's younger partner and most important helper! Wonder Girl is Wonder Woman's sidekick. Speedy is Green Arrow's sidekick.

sign

Look out below! A super-villain has knocked down a **sign**!

sing

The super heroes **sing** "Happy Birthday."

skirt

Supergirl wears a red **skirt**.

sky

Wonder Woman flies through the **sky** near her Invisible Jet.

skyscraper

A **skyscraper** is a very tall building.

slide

The little boy loves to **slide**. It's not safe to slide on the roof. He should slide at the playground.

slip

It's easy to **slip** on ice if you're not careful.

smart

Mr. Mind is **smart** because he reads a lot.

smile

You can tell from Starfire's **smile** that she feels happy.

snap

It takes practice to **snap** your fingers just like The Flash.

SNAP

sneak

Mirror Master is trying to **sneak** away without being seen!

snow

Even super heroes bundle up when it **snows**.

snowball

With a **snowball** that big, Wonder Woman could make a giant snowman!

spill

The Flash **spilled** his lunch tray!

splash

Aquaman leaps from the ocean with a big **splash**.

spot

Cheetah's costume is covered with **spots**.

square

Instead of being round like planet Earth, Bizarro World is **square**.

squeeze

Copperhead **squeezes** too hard when he hugs.

stand

Batgirl **stands** tall.

star

The night sky is filled with **stars**.

S s

statue

The people of Metropolis say "thank you" to Superman by putting up a **statue**.

SUPERMAN

ERECTED BY THE CITIZENS OF METROPOLIS IN GRATEFUL RECOGNITION OF HIS MANY SERVICES TO THE COMMUNITY AND TO MANKIND

steering wheel
Batman uses the **steering wheel** to control the Batmobile.

storm
A big lightning **storm** lights up the sky.

street
Batgirl zooms down the **street** on her motorcycle.

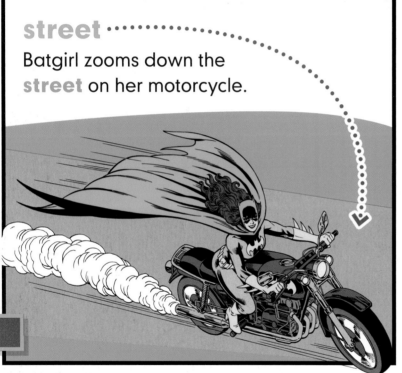

streetlight
A **streetlight** helps drivers see where they are going at night.

stripe
Trickster's costume has lots of **stripes**.

strong

John Stewart is **strong** because he has lots of muscles.

stuck

Green Lantern cannot pull his ring off the power battery. It is **stuck**!

suitcase

When Superboy goes on a trip, he packs his clothes in a **suitcase**.

sun

The **sun** rises behind the city.

sunset

Sunset is the time at the end of the day when the sun disappears.

S s

superpower

A **superpower** is a special ability that no one has in real life. The Elongated Man's superpower is being able to stretch his body.

Supergirl

Supergirl has the same powers as her famous cousin, Superman.

Superman

Superman is sometimes called the Man of Steel.

surprise

A super-villain is **surprised** when Superman outsmarts him again.

sweat

We **sweat** when it is hot or when we exercise.

swim

The baby goes for a **swim**.

swing

Batgirl **swings** on a rope.

S s

tail

Copperhead has a long **tail**.

talk

Clark Kent **talks** with a friend.

tall

Elongated Man can be very **tall**.

tangle

The Riddler has got Batman and Robin **tangled** up.

T t

102

target

Green Arrow always hits his **target**.

teacher

Aquaman's **teacher** thinks he is very clever.

AMAZING! SIMPLY AMAZING!

team

When super heroes work together, they become a powerful **team**.

T t

Teen Titans

The **Teen Titans** are just as strong and brave as the grown-up heroes.

teeth

Aquaman's smile is bright because he never forgets to brush his **teeth**.

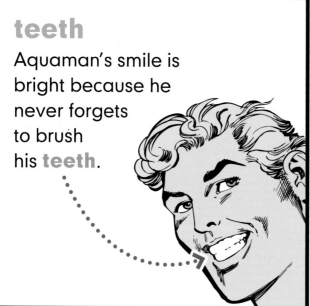

television

Bruce Wayne and Dick Grayson watch a news report on **television**.

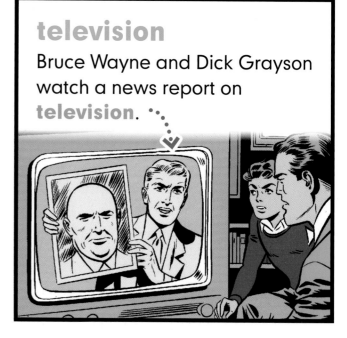

tennis

The Flash is fast enough to play **tennis** against himself!

tent

Superman flies high above a circus **tent**.

throw

The Flash can **throw** a baseball at super-speed.

tiger

Animal Man dances with a wild **tiger**.

through

The Flash has the power to pass right **through** solid walls!

tiara

Wonder Woman wears a golden **tiara** on her head.

tilt

Batgirl's motorcycle **tilts** to one side.

T t

tiny

People and cars look like **tiny** specks when Superman flies this high in the air.

tiptoe

Harley Quinn sneaks past on **tiptoe**.

tired

Lifting mountains all day makes Shazam! feel **tired**.

together

Batman, Robin, and Batgirl fight crime **together**.

tool

Tools hang on the wall behind young Clark Kent.

T t

toy chest

A **toy chest** is a great place to put your toys.

train

Shazam! will get that **train** back on track.

train tracks

The train is supposed to run on the **train tracks**.

treasure

This explorer is excited to find a hidden **treasure**!

T t

tree

Wonder Woman flies her Invisible Jet next to a tall **tree**.

tricycle

A **tricycle** has three wheels and is fun to ride at any speed.

truck

Superman takes a big **truck** for a ride.

tunnel

Superboy digs an underground **tunnel**.

turtle

The baby plays with a sea **turtle**.

U

uh-oh

Uh-oh! Superman pulled too hard on that door!

umbrella

The Penguin carries his **umbrella** even when it isn't raining.

under

Red Tornado runs **under** Green Lantern.

U u

up

If the people of Gotham City look **up**, they might see Batman swing past the rooftops.

upside down

Shazam! flies **upside down**.

use

Hawkgirl **uses** a pole to tame a dragon.

Utility Belt

Batman keeps all sorts of useful things in his **Utility Belt**.

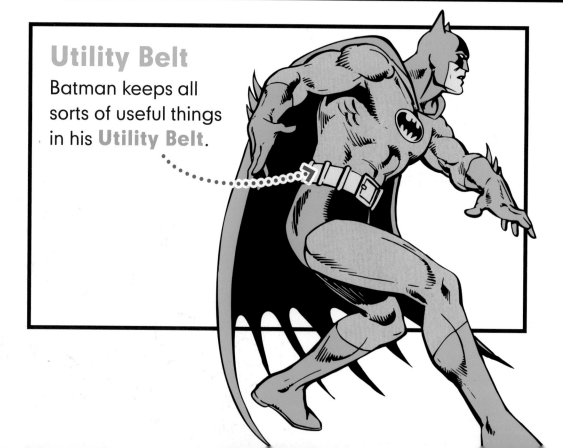

U u

V

very

An anglerfish has **very** long teeth.

view

Elongated Man has a good **view** of the whole city.

NICE GOING, RALPH! BUT YOU'D BETTER COME DOWN NOW BEFORE THEY SPOT YOU!

villain

Watch out for these **villains**— they can be very naughty!

V v

W

walk

A woman goes for a **walk** in the city.

warm

His fuzzy hood and gloves keep this super-villain **warm**.

waterfall

Water rushes down over a cliff in this enormous **waterfall**.

wave

Here comes a giant **wave**!

W w

wave

The Flash says hello with a friendly **wave**.

wet

Wonder Woman is all **wet**.

whale

The big **whale** shoots water from its blowhole.

wheel

The **wheels** on the Batmobile go round and round!

wheelchair

This man uses a **wheelchair** to move around.

whisper

Lois Lane **whispers** a secret to Jimmy Olsen.

W w

wide

Doctor Fate spreads his arms **wide**.

wind

Batman's cape blows all over in the **wind**.

window

Wonder Woman looks out the **window**.

wings

Hawkgirl flies through the air on powerful **wings**.

wink

Clark Kent **winks** when he closes then opens one eye.

Wonder Girl

Wonder Girl has learned great rope tricks from Wonder Woman.

Wonder Woman

Wonder Woman is famous for both her strength and her kindness.

worried

The Joker looks **worried** because he's about to get in trouble.

write

Use a pencil and paper to **write** a note.

W w

X

X-ray

Superman uses his **X-ray** vision to see through anything.

young

When he was **young**, Superman knew how to fly but not how to land!

yummy

When the adventure is over, it's time for **yummy** cake!

Y y

Z

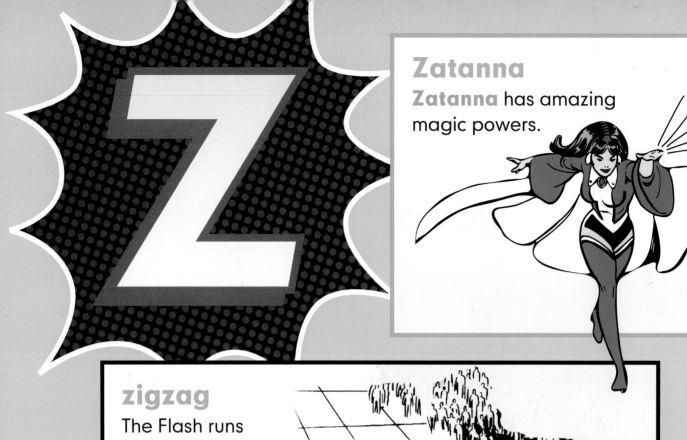

Zatanna
Zatanna has amazing magic powers.

zigzag
The Flash runs back and forth in a **zigzag** pattern.

zoom
Aquaman **zooms** ahead of a speedboat.

Z z

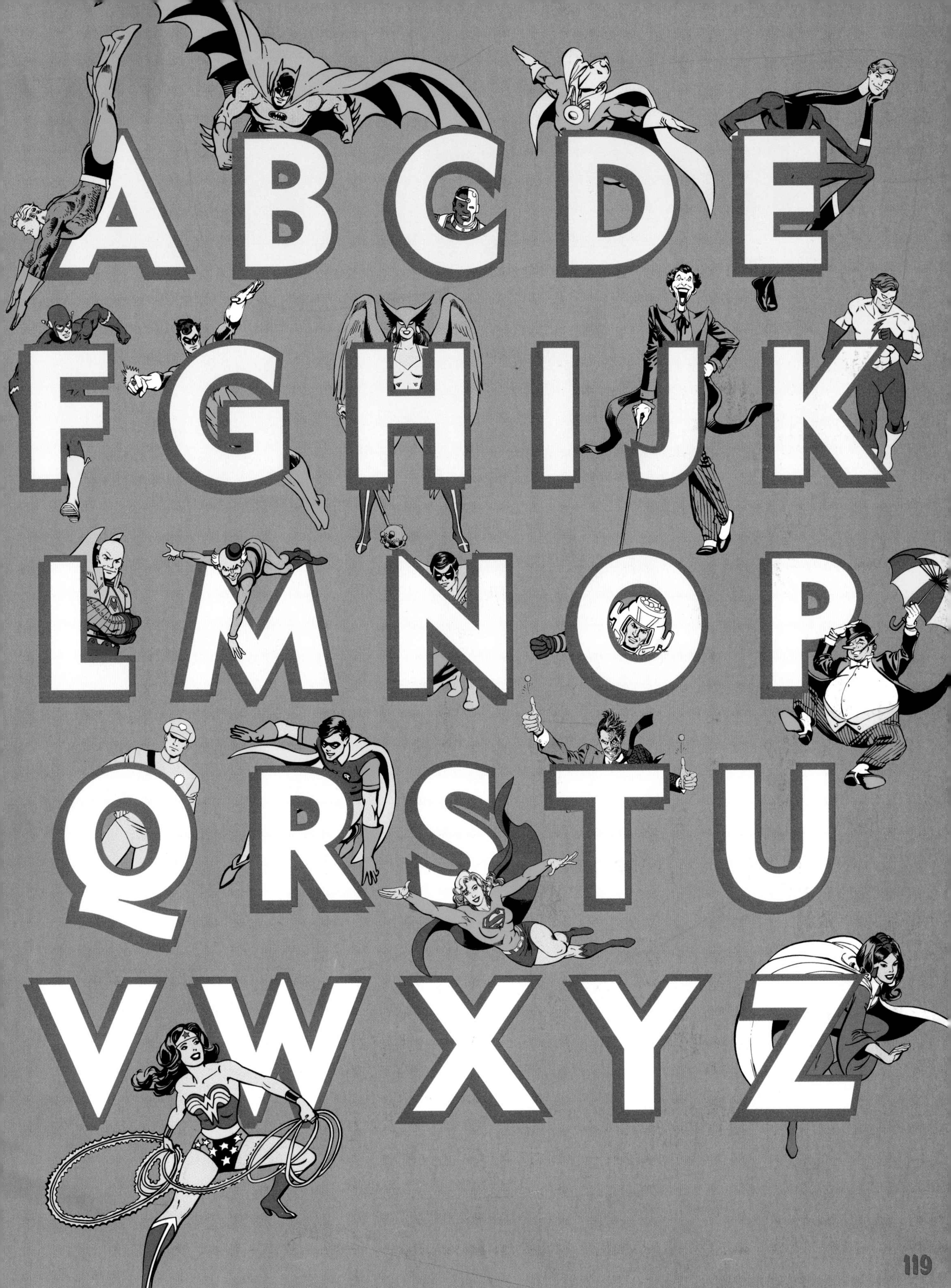
ABCDE
FGHIJK
LMNOP
QRSTU
VWXYZ

STRONG BODIES

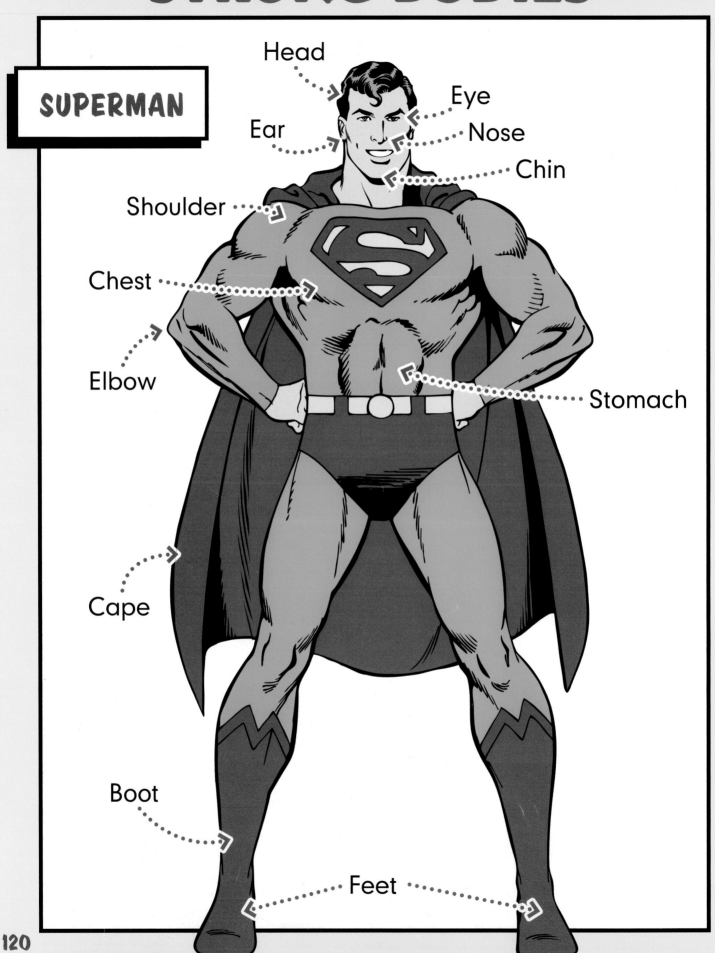

SUPERMAN

Head
Eye
Nose
Ear
Chin
Shoulder
Chest
Elbow
Stomach
Cape
Boot
Feet

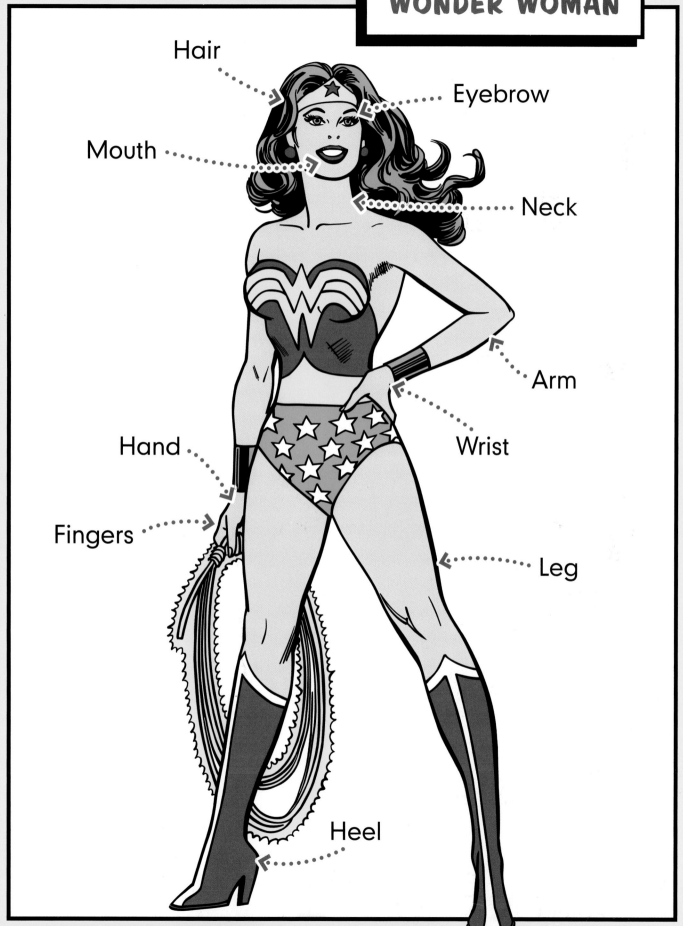

Hair

Eyebrow

Mouth

Neck

Arm

Hand

Wrist

Fingers

Leg

Heel

GOING PLACES

AIRPLANE

BOAT

CAR

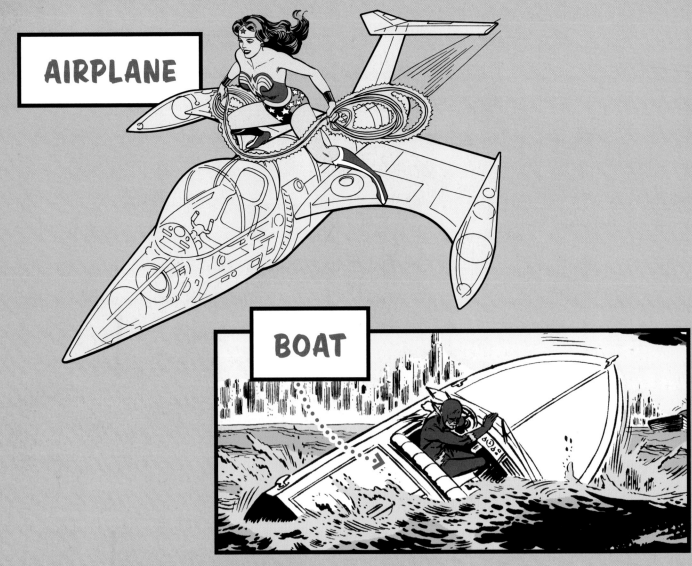

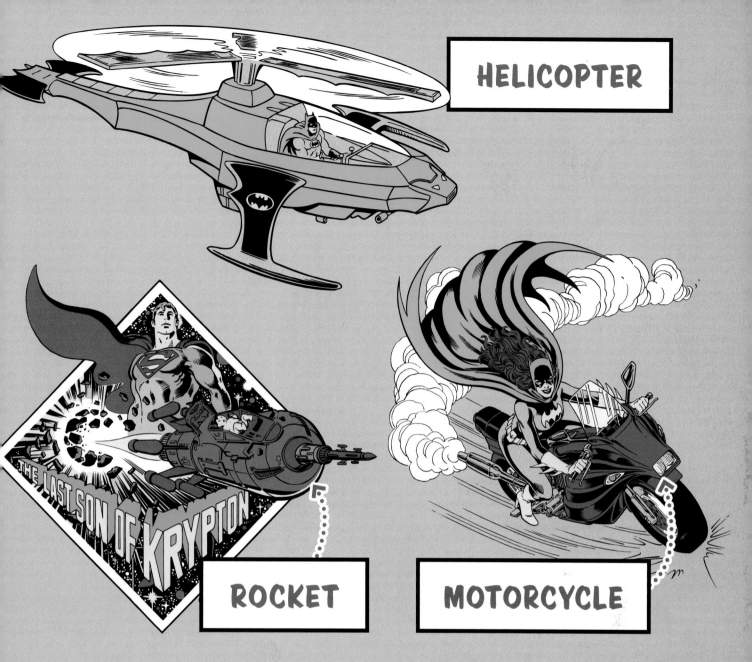

HELICOPTER

ROCKET

THE LAST SON OF KRYPTON

MOTORCYCLE

SUBMARINE

WHO IS FAMILY?

PARENTS

Jor-El and Lara are Superman's Kryptonian father and mother.

Martha and Jonathan Kent are Superman's adoptive parents here on Earth.

COUSINS

Superman and Supergirl have different parents but are from the same family. They are cousins.

HUSBAND AND WIFE

Aquaman and Mera are married to each other. They are husband and wife.

BROTHER AND SISTER

Shazam! and Mary have the same mom and dad. Shazam! is Mary's brother. Mary is Shazam!'s sister.

FATHER AND DAUGHTER

Commissioner Gordon is Batgirl's father. She is his daughter.

MOTHER AND SON

A proud mother looks out to sea. Her son will grow up to be Aquaman!

COLORS AND NUMBERS

1 One orange robot

2 Two purple hats

3 Three green power rings

4 Four brown wings

5 Five blue gloves

6 Six black bat-symbols

7 Seven red eyes

8 Eight yellow belts

9 Nine red boots

10

Ten colorful
super heroes!